Gross-Out Defenses

Disgusting HAGFISH

by Meish Goldish

Consultants:
Gabrielle Sachs, Zoo Educator
Mike Mincarone, Ichthyologist

BEARPORT
PUBLISHING

NEW YORK, NEW YORK

Credits

Cover, © Tom Stack/Tom Stack & Associates; TOC, © Tom Stack/Tom Stack & Associates; 4, © SeaPics.com; 5, © Brandon D. Cole/Corbis; 6, © Karen Petersen; 7, © Emory Kristof/National Geographic/Getty Images; 8, © Norbert Wu/Norbert Wu Productions; 9, © Brandon D. Cole/Corbis; 10, © C. Ortlepp; 11, © Tom McHugh/Photo Researchers, Inc.; 12, © Brandon D. Cole/Brandon Cole Marine Photography; 13, © Tom Stack/Tom Stack & Associates; 14, © Steven Kazlowski/Peter Arnold Inc.; 15, © Dennis Wilson/Pangaea Designs; 17, © blickwinkel/Hecker/Alamy; 18, © SeaPics.com; 19, © SeaPics.com; 20, © Brandon D. Cole/Corbis; 21, © Peter Batson/Image Quest Marine; 22, © Wolfgang Pölzer/Alamy; 23TL, © Tom Stack/Tom Stack & Associates; 23TR, © Stuart Dow/Shutterstock; 23BL, © Kristian Sekulic/Shutterstock; 23BR, © Brandon D. Cole/Corbis.

Publisher: Kenn Goin
Senior Editor: Lisa Wiseman
Creative Director: Spencer Brinker
Design: Becky Munich
Photo Researcher: Amy Dunleavy

Library of Congress Cataloging-in-Publication Data

Goldish, Meish.
  Disgusting hagfish / by Meish Goldish.
      p. cm. —(Gross-out defenses)
  Includes bibliographical references and index.
  ISBN-13: 978-1-59716-719-2 (library binding)
  ISBN-10: 1-59716-719-3 (library binding)
  1. Hagfishes—Juvenile literature. 2. Animal defenses—Juvenile literature. I. Title.

  QL638.14.G65 2009
  597'.2—dc22
                              2008008624

For more information, write to Bearport Publishing Company, Inc., 101 Fifth Avenue, Suite 6R, New York, New York 10003. Printed in the United States of America.

10 9 8 7 6 5 4 3 2 1

Contents

A Yucky Mess

As it hunts for its next meal, an octopus sees an animal that looks like a snake.

However, the snake is really a hagfish.

The scared hagfish quickly shoots white **slime** at the octopus.

The slime turns thick and sticky in the water.

The stinky, gooey mess makes it hard for the octopus to breathe.

It barely escapes alive.

octopus

Hagfish are also known as *slime hags* or *slime eels*. Scientists call them the most disgusting animals in the ocean because of their sticky goo.

slime

hagfish

Slime Time

A hagfish is always making slime inside its body.

It pushes out the sticky goo when it's in danger.

The slime shoots out of tiny holes, called pores, in the fish's skin.

The milky slime clouds the water, making it hard for an enemy to see the hagfish.

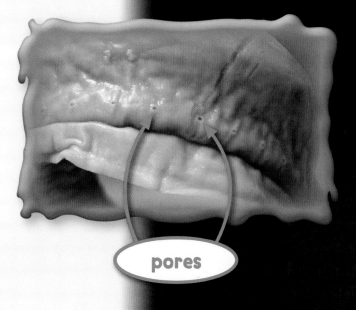

pores

A hagfish's slime increases when it mixes with seawater. Minutes after a hagfish shoots out its slime, there's enough goo to fill a seven-quart (7-l) bucket.

Deadly Goo

Slime from a hagfish can kill an enemy.

In the water, the goo clogs the enemy's **gills**.

This makes it very hard for the creature to breathe.

If the slimed enemy doesn't swim away from the goo quickly enough, it dies.

Few sea animals are brave enough to attack hagfish. Seabirds, codfish, porpoises, and dolphins, however, don't fear this disgusting creature.

hagfish slime

hagfish

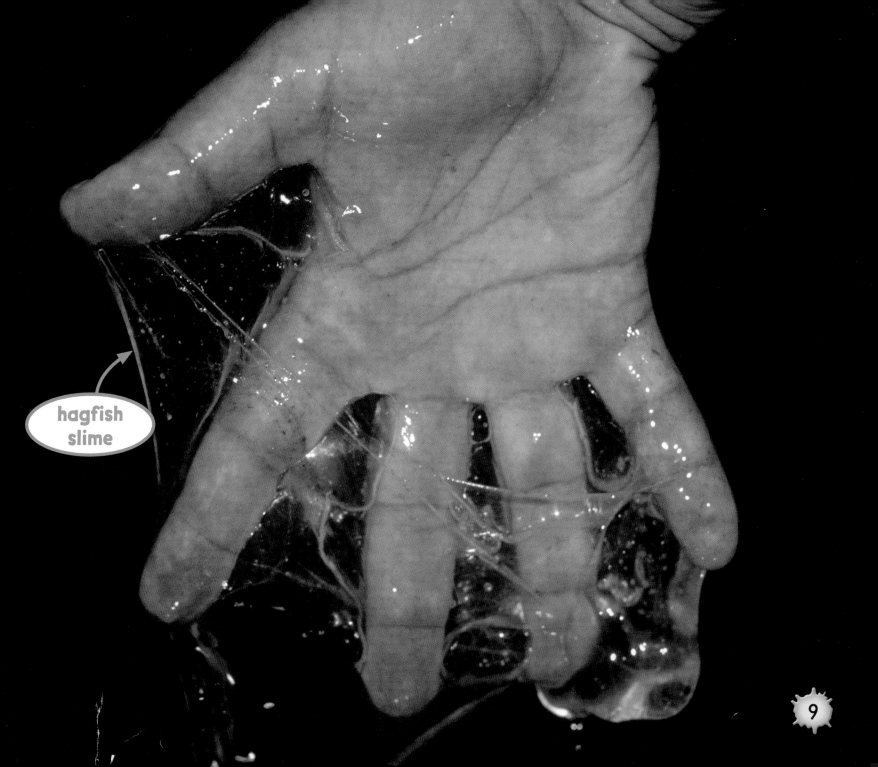

hagfish slime

9

Knot Now

When a hagfish slimes an enemy, it also gets slime on itself.

The hagfish has a trick, though, to get rid of the goo on its own body.

The long thin fish ties itself into a knot.

Then it moves in and out of the knot.

This action wipes off the slime.

hagfish in a knot

Slime can even clog a hagfish's nose. The animal gets rid of it by sneezing.

nose

Slip and Slide

Slime doesn't just protect a hagfish, it also helps it get food.

A hagfish hunts for sick or dead animals on the ocean floor.

When a hagfish spots its **prey**, it slimes itself to make its body slippery.

Then it can squeeze inside the animal through a body opening, such as the mouth.

Why does it do this?

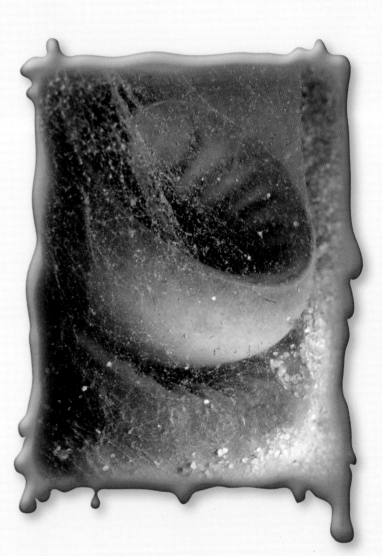

A hagfish doesn't have eyes so it can't see. It finds prey by using its good sense of smell and by feeling around as it swims. It has several **feelers** around its mouth to help it find food.

feelers

Eating In

A hagfish squeezes inside its prey's body because it mostly eats its meals from the inside out.

It doesn't have jaws for chewing food.

Instead, a hagfish sucks on meat inside an animal's dead body.

When it's done eating, all that's left of the prey is skin and bones!

Hagfish are not liked by fishermen. Often, they eat the fishermen's catch before their nets can be pulled out of the ocean.

14

hagfish eating

Around the World

There are about 70 different kinds of hagfish.

They live in oceans all around the world.

They swim in water that is cold and salty.

Most hagfish stay near the ocean floor, where they can find food.

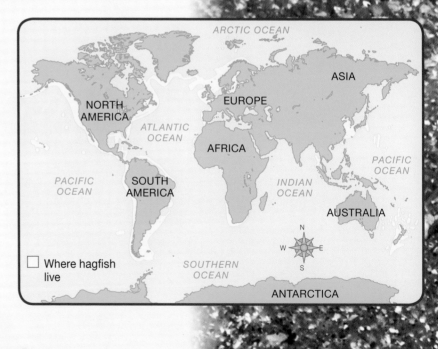

ARCTIC OCEAN

ASIA

EUROPE

NORTH
AMERICA

ATLANTIC
OCEAN

AFRICA

PACIFIC
OCEAN

PACIFIC
OCEAN

SOUTH
AMERICA

INDIAN
OCEAN

AUSTRALIA

N

W   E

S

☐ Where hagfish
live

SOUTHERN
OCEAN

ANTARCTICA

Some hagfish live really deep in the ocean—as far down as 9,186 feet (2,800 m). That's almost 2 miles (3.2 km) below sea level.

A Muddy Home

Most hagfish live in burrows at the bottom of the ocean.

A burrow is a hole or tunnel made by an animal to live in.

The hagfish pushes itself into the soft mud to shape its home.

This home doesn't last for long, though.

The burrow caves in when the hagfish leaves.

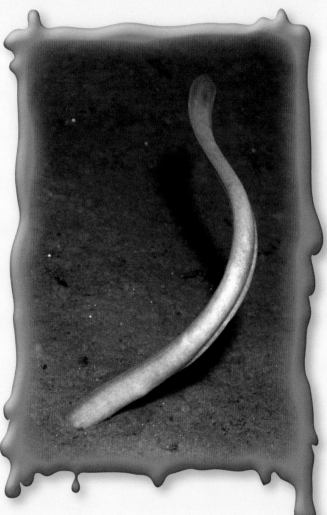

Hagfish live in large groups. Up to 15,000 of these creatures may live close together in one small part of the ocean. Each one, however, has its own burrow.

Baby Hagfish

Though a hagfish lives in a burrow, it doesn't lay its eggs there.

A mother hagfish lays her eggs in soft mud on the ocean floor.

She lays about 25 eggs at a time.

When first born, a hagfish looks like its parents, only smaller.

Soon the babies will be ready to ooze their own disgusting slime!

eggs

Hagfish eggs have threads attached to them that stick to the ocean floor. So the eggs are able to stay in one place until they hatch.

Another Slimy Defense

Hagfish aren't the only animals that use slime to stay safe. A clown fish is a type of fish that is covered in slime. This goo protects it from the deadly stings of a sticky sea animal called an anemone (uh-NEM-uh-nee). When the anemone touches the slime of the clown fish, it thinks it's touching itself. It can't tell the difference between its own stickiness and the clown fish's slime. So the sea animal doesn't sting the clown fish.

clown fish

anemone

Glossary

feelers
(FEEL-urz)
the body parts
near a hagfish's
mouth that help
it find food

gills (GILZ) body
parts that help fish
breathe underwater

prey (PRAY)
an animal that is
hunted by another
animal for food

slime (SLIME)
a soft, slippery goo
made by hagfish
to keep them safe
from enemies

Index

Read More

Everts, Tammy, and Bobbie Kalman. *Really Weird Animals*. New York: Crabtree Publishing (1995).

Morgan, Sally. *Fish.* Chicago: Raintree (2005).

Zim, Herbert, and Hurst Shoemaker. *Fishes.* New York: Golden Books (1987).

Learn More Online

To learn more about hagfish, visit
www.bearportpublishing.com/GrossOutDefenses

About the Author

Meish Goldish has written more than 100 books for children. He lives in Brooklyn, New York, where no hagfish has ever slimed him.